A Theory of Power

A Theory of Power

Jeff Vail

iUniverse, Inc.

New York Lincoln Shanghai

A Theory of Power

iUniverse, Inc.

For information address:
iUniverse, Inc.
2021 Pine Lake Road, Suite 100
Lincoln, NE 68512
www.iuniverse.com

ISBN: 0-595-33030-4

Printed in the United States of America

For Tom Hudspeth, who first taught me to question.

Contents

Preface

or something else? [handwritten annotation]

I began writing this book while puzzling about the nature of power. I was debating the cause of the state of the world: is our present situation the result of some mysterious conspiracy, or is it the logical result of natural processes of power? As I looked into the nature of power, it became increasingly clear that the prominent actors and forces in the world today are emergent phenomena, resulting from a dominant, hierarchal pattern of power. The structure of power, it seems, is the root cause of the problems humanity struggles to solve. The result of my inquiry—this Theory of Power—is my attempt to understand root causes and to present a toolkit addressing the daunting problems facing our civilization.

The first eight chapters outline my theory as it parallels the development of civilization and humanity. The ninth chapter provides my suggested tools to solve the problems presented. The goal of this book is to both present the world in a new and revealing way, and to provide suggestions that inspire the reader with implementable solutions.

I would also like to take this opportunity to grant blanket permission to reproduce and use any portion of this text for any non-commercial purpose. I hope that the message of this book reaches as large an audience as possible—and for that, I request your support.

Jeff Vail
Colorado—August 22, 2004

1

Introduction: A Theory of Power

I have often wondered about the structure of the world. What drives our actions and desires? Why do patterns appear to repeat themselves throughout history? Why do the poor outnumber the rich? Can I find the blueprints for the world laid out in some cosmic instruction manual—if not, then what forces have defined its course of development? Simply looking at the surface of the world around me has never provided satisfying answers. Stemming from my desire to understand myself and my environment, I have attempted to understand the fabric of so-called "reality," from the microscopic to the cosmic—how and why it works the way it does. In the process, I have come to understand the difference between perception and truth. I have realized that truth "is" a perception, just as much as anything "is" at all.[1] The irrational assumption, the belief in the sanctity of "is" seems to form the foundation of our mask of reality.

For thousands of years, sages and mystics of many religions have questioned this impression of reality. They call reality "Maya", an illusion. To Buddhists, Christian Gnostics or Sufi Muslims, the path to enlightenment requires one to see through this illusion.[2] The scientific community rejected this uncertainty and presented an opposing picture of reality. Following the examples of Galileo and Newton, scientists defined the world "objectively"—look closely enough, they

---

1.   I have written this text, almost entirely, in the language of 'English Prime'—English, without the "is of identity", as proposed by Alfred Korzybski—in fact, without any form of the verb "to be", as proposed by David Bourland, R.A. Wilson and others. This results, hopefully, in a more operational language. It avoids the irrational, dogmatic mannerism of stating that something "is" something else, without providing any further justification to equate the two terms than the mere presence of the verb "to be". The few exceptions, noted in quotation marks, are used primarily to point out the logical fallacy of the verb "to be".

2.   For an outstanding overview of the world's spiritual traditions, see Aldous Huxley's "The Perennial Philosophy"

said, and a concrete structure, an absolute deep-reality emerges. In the 20th century, however, developments in the field of quantum mechanics, anthropology and psychology began to support a consilience of science and mysticism—they suggest that both views appear correct, even inseparable.

Consilience, the unification of varied fields of scientific inquiry, pushed aside the veil of illusion to reveal the foundations of reality.[3] Reality, it turns out, often appears as anything but static, instead appearing as a dynamic web of transactional entities and experiences. Strikingly, experiments continue to suggest that everything in the universe influences every other thing, instantaneously, and at all times.[4] Reductionism—defining the smallest component particles of existence—will not illuminate the nature of our world. Rather, the connections, the power-relationships between entities prove illuminating, coalescing to form the "tangible" around us. *It's a whole*

The networks of connections, not the elements connected, appear to constitute a more accurate map of reality. Consider this a critical paradigm shift: *the connections, not the parties connected, may best represent our world.* Take the seemingly simple nature of this very book. All of our senses confirm that it "is" a solid object, with little mysterious about it. Another of our models of reality represents its composition as that of a web of billions of atoms; nearly entirely empty space speckled with clusters of sub-atomic particles. Other models exclude the concept of a concrete "particle" entirely: quantum mechanics provides us with a model of reality without fixed particles at all, using instead a nebulous web of constantly changing energies and waves of probability. These energies and connections may represent all that actually exists! The connections, the power-relationships between perceived "entities" make up the world around us, not the illusion of particles. This concept of the connection, and the power-relationship it represents, extends to our genes, our culture and our technology. It wields great power over all areas of our lives. Our thoughts, desires and self-perceptions, our very

---

3. See Edward O. Wilson's "Consilience: The Unity of Knowledge"
4. R. A. Wilson summarizes Dr. John S. Bell's 1965 theorem: "If some sort of objective universe exists in some sense…and, if the equations of quantum mechanics have a similarity of structure (isomorphism) to that universe, then, some sort of non-local correlation exists between any two particles that ever came in contact" (Quantum Psychology, pg. 167). In other words, any two things that ever came in contact will always maintain an instantaneous influence on each other, no matter how distant the separation between them. The far-reaching implications of this theorem demonstrate the importance of *connections* to the functioning of our universe.

identity, stems from this enigmatic web of connectivity. This book will explore the concept of the connection, the power-relationship, as it underlies the fabric of reality.

A closer examination of the dynamics, structure and evolution of patterns of connections will provide the foundation for exploring and learning to work with power-relationships. The complex web of connectivity animating our world did not simply spring into existence fully formed. Rather this web results from the ongoing processes of development and intensification. Understanding the process of how and why we have arrived at our present state provides the insight that will eventually give us greater control over our future. It will illuminate the fundamental clockwork of our minds, bodies and societies, revealing principles of power-relationships that govern all aspects of what we perceive as reality, from the environment and economics to politics and psychology. It will unravel the bonds that hold humanity in slavery to the patterns of history—and ultimately provide the key to our freedom. Understanding the interconnectivity of such diverse fields will yield a theory of power-relationships that will expand our understanding of the world as a whole. This theory will reduce power to its discrete nature and reassemble it into the swirling web that exists around us. Power defines every aspect of our experience of reality. Ultimately, this knowledge, this theory of power, will provide us with a tool chest to affect our world.

2

The Structure of Evolution

Good definition

I define a "power-relationship" as the ability of one entity to influence the action of another entity. Such relationships appear to exist across all scales. One can view people, companies or governments as single, coherent entities exerting influence on others. One can also interpret each as a network of internal entities and power-relationships from which the whole emerges. For example, one can model a simple oxygen atom as a vast array of power relationships, with strong forces holding together a variety of elusive quarks to form protons and neutrons, and weak forces constraining electrons to certain regions of possible location. Even the simplest particles appear as no more than a stable pattern of energy and power.[1] Work at the frontiers of physics suggests that discrete particles exist as nothing more than a construct of the observer: that the true fabric of reality lies in the *connection*, and that the particles connected appear as an illusion. Connections assemble into patterns and networks, forming everything around us. On any scale, from the sub-atomic to the global, understanding the behavior of the coherent whole requires an understanding of the underlying networks of connections, the networks of power-relationships.

Exactly how the universe came into being remains an uncertainty, but most physicists and astronomers today agree that the present state came about through a long period of particle evolution—energies and interactions coalescing and colliding to form new, more complex entities. If new patterns of forces could survive their impacts with one another, if they tended to hold together rather than tear

---

1. For an excellent, accessible introduction to quantum physics and wave-particle duality, read "The Dancing Wu Li Masters" by Gary Zukav. For a more technical coverage of the topic, see "QED: The Strange Theory of Light and Matter" by Richard Feynman. For the truly adventurous, those interested in the most current theories on the birth and death of "particles" from energy, see "Quantum Field Theory in a Nutshell" by Anthony Zee (2003).

apart, then they represented a stable collection of power-relationships. They survived. Other patterns lasted only millionths of a second before breaking apart or being consumed by outside forces. Such patterns of connection appear to self-organize, not through some conscious design, but through one simple rule: if random events lead to the creation of a stable complex of power-relationships, then that entity persists.

Today, particle accelerators provide scientists with a tool to study the dance of sub-atomic energies. Sub-atomic physicists consider it critical to understand the component power-relationships of even simple elements in order to predict characteristics of the element as a whole. With a particle accelerator, the addition of great outside forces (the force required to accelerate one particle to collision with another at high speed) overcomes the inherent stability of the power-relationships inside the particle. This collision provides physicists with the opportunity to briefly peer inside the works of a seemingly monolithic entity and catch a glimpse of the underlying web of connections. By observing how sub-atomic entities and energies interact, we gain the capability to better understand the forces that animate and define the coherent atom. The same concept of power-relationships that defines sub-atomic structure also seems to define the larger world we live in—ecologies, societies and economies. It acts like opening the back of a watch to reveal the works inside. When we realize the illusion of monolithic structures, that everything actually appears composed of internal and external networks of connections, we gain a much more useful understanding of the nature of the world around us. Breaking down complex entities to observe and learn about their component power-relationships provides the knowledge, the power to influence the world.

Deconstruction serves as a key to understanding systemic evolution—the rules and processes by which everything constantly changes, replicates and interacts. Most people express a general familiarity with evolution from the teachings of Charles Darwin and the evolution of biological organisms. Here we will use a broader interpretation; one that applies to much more than just biology. This interpretation suggests a dynamic nature of everything—entirely inanimate entities, societies, economies, all governed by the same basic principles that define biology.[2] The attempt to get to the root structure of nature must focus on this

---

2.   The concept is explored in depth in *1000 Years of Non-Linear History* by Manuel de Landa. One of his many examples of dynamic nature—that of a sand dune—is presented later in this chapter.

broader, systemic view of evolution, and its two key components: self-replication and natural selection.

I define self-replication as the process by which one pattern of power-relationships, whether a molecule, computer virus or management style, causes the reproduction of itself.[3] The mechanism of reproduction may vary, from the genetic reproduction process of living organisms to conscious mimicry, as demonstrated by the imitation of a successful management style. The salient point remains that some patterns of power-relationships demonstrate the quality of self-replication, regardless of the actual mechanics by which they accomplish replication.

The second core process, natural selection, has close ties to the process of self-replication. When several self-replicating entities exist in the same environment, their ongoing reproduction will eventually run into a limited supply of some resource that they all require. Regardless of what the required "resource" may consist of (i.e. money, food, electrons, attention, etc.), the specific pattern-entity most capable of obtaining or utilizing that scarce resource will most likely survive. It will self-replicate more than, and at the expense of, less capable patterns of power-relationships.

Every entity, every pattern of power-relationships, demonstrates dependence on some type of resource for survival, maintenance and reproduction. The self-replicating nature of most such entities creates a dynamic environment of competition for scarce resources. In competition, one pattern in particular has proven exceptionally successful: imperfect replication. Self-replicating entities often fail to create a perfect copy of themselves. This creates variation, or mutation, in the originating pattern. Often the mutation fails miserably in the fight for scarce resources. Sometimes, however, a slightly different pattern has far more success than the original. The process of imperfect replication leads to the evolution of entities that exhibit ever greater capability in their quest for resources.[4]

---

3.   Other examples include the turbulent flow of fluids, cells creating structured tissue and fish forming into schools. For an in-depth look at self-replication, see "Self-Organization in Biological Systems" by Scott Camazine, et al.
4.   It has been suggested, by Alan Turing among others, that to simulate something is to truly understand it. If true, then there can be few better books on understanding evolution than John Holland's *A Hidden Order*. Holland explains incipient life by providing a step-by-step guide to its simulation.

[handwritten margin notes: "They don't self-replicate — people replicate them"; "ok — natural selection works"; "That's still improvement with new ideas"; "That's still existing context and..."]

The fact that one can see the process of evolution itself as an example of patterns and power-relationships demonstrates just how broadly the concepts apply. Fundamental methods of organization, such as hierarchy and rhizome—topics we will revisit later—also serve as examples of patterns of power-relationships. We can view everything in our world, traditionally divided between "living" and "non-living", through a new lens of perception. Now we can see that what once appeared as nothing more than a static object or abstract concept now consists of an entity emerging from the dynamic competition for scarce resources.

Take this lens and reconsider the nature of everything around you. What constitutes a catchy tune, a new expression, a popular business practice or an innovative military technique? Of the thousands of new businesses created each year, those that exhibit the most economic fitness will tend to survive the selection process, proving more capable of replicating (or expanding) themselves (as will their component business practices). Look to nature: sand dunes, for example, represent an even more abstract illustration of self-replication—they appear as shapes that can act like life forms. Some dunes will channel turbulent wind flows to continuously increase the size of the dune. Other dune shapes will create vortexes that propagate a chain of repetitive dunes extending off from the first. These spectacular dunes consist only superficially of particles of sand. Dig deeper and it becomes clear that their essential substance consists of a network of connections, a pattern of power-relationships. Sand and wind merely represent resources that this entity harnesses. The organizing pattern itself most essentially defines their identity.[5] The pattern-entity of a sand dune serves as an example of a "body without organs", the concept that the organizing process, the underlying pattern of power relationships represents the true essence and identity of anything.[6] There exist nearly endless examples of how the lens of pattern and power-relationship can provide new insight and understanding of the world. We will follow patterns of

---

5.   Major Ralph Bagnold, working in the Sahara for the British Royal Signals in the 1930's, commented that "Dunes are mobile heaps of sand whose existence is independent of either ground form or fixed wind obstruction. They appear to retain their shape and identity indefinitely, and so have an interesting life of their own."

6.   "[A] body without organs, which is continually dismantling the organism, causing asignifying particles of pure intensities to pass or circulate, and attributing to itself subjects that it leaves with nothing more than a name as a trace of an intensity." This is the definition of 'a body without organs' in the words of its inventor, Gilles Deleuze. It is one of the key concepts of Deleuzian philosophy, more of which will be discussed in Chapter IX. Cited from "A Thousand Plateaus" by Gilles Deleuze and Felix Guattari, pg 4.

power down the rabbit hole to see if they change our understanding of ourselves, and of reality.

The approach of deconstructing something to reveal its underlying connections serves as a useful tool in the examination of patterns of biological self and ego, as well as those patterns that we have become a part of: our societies, economic and political structures and concepts of spirituality. We will take a developmental, historical approach in the deconstruction of our world. In order to provide any value, this deconstruction must yield an understanding that improves the efficacy of our actions. With the prevalence of dynamic processes in this model, it appears necessary to understand a process' ontogeny, its evolutionary development and progression *from the past* in order to affect its development in the future. Such understanding represents a step toward the construction of tools to attack essential problems of philosophy: How do we define ourselves? What do we want? What should we see as our role in life? If we can resolve these questions, and gain greater understanding of patterns and power-relationships, we can apply this knowledge toward realizing our visions of the future.

3

The Interplay of Genetics and Culture

[handwritten margin note: Self-replication is the prerequisite for natural selection to work. But that is not evolution]

[handwritten margin note: where is that from?]

[handwritten margin note: ?]

Roughly 4 billion years ago, the beginnings of what we call "life" appeared on Earth. Self-replication and natural selection facilitated the evolution of increasingly complex molecular patterns, eventually allowing simple organisms to develop and pass on information encoded in molecular patterns such as the DNA molecule. These genetic patterns formed the basis for all biological life on our planet. The standard evolutionary story continues that, over time, patterns coalesced into discrete genes—tools used by each species to effectively combine and reproduce. This story now appears incorrect: genes do not behave as servants to their respective species, as they are so often represented. As Richard Dawkins explained in his 1979 book *The Selfish Gene*, the organism does not use the gene to reproduce itself. The gene, rather, uses the organism as a host for reproduction. This creates a subtle, yet critical difference—the *gene* exerts control over the organism in this power-relationship. Many people experience this as a startling realization that our genes use us as tools—the gene controls us!

[handwritten margin note: who uses the genes?]

Our genes exercise power over us through a variety of methods. We are genetically programmed to act in ways that have proven beneficial to the gene, if not necessarily beneficial to us, the hosts. At the most basic level, the gene exercises power by carefully programming our instincts, via the structure of our brain chemistry, to ensure its survival. Sexual desire, for example, serves as a tool of our genes. Physical pleasure from the act of procreation increases its occurrence, improving the rate of reproduction, thereby ensuring propagation of the associated genes. This theory views sexual pleasure as a method that passed the test of natural selection—it exists and prospers because it works so well. Similarly, the fight-or-flight responses, hard-wired into the human nervous system, exist because they have proven their ability to prolong life. The response increases the

[handwritten note at bottom: It doesn't mean that it is there because natural selection favoured it and thus brought it life]

chance of an individual reaching reproductive age, which leads to propagation and the survival of the host's genes.

Genes do not consciously plan out their survival strategies. Their development follows the basic mechanics of natural selection: if a random mutation in a gene makes an individual more likely to survive and reproduce, then the associated gene will more likely increase its frequency in the gene pool. Environmental constraints and the competition for scarce resources limit the number of individuals that can survive to reproduce. Over time, those individuals who demonstrate greater capacity for survival due to changes in their genes will replace those with less genetic fitness.

As mental capacity increased with the evolution of higher order animals, new types of power-relationships evolved. Many animals do not live in isolation; they live in small groups or communities on which they depend for survival, or the opportunity to mate. Developing in a group setting, genes proved more likely to prosper if they evolved mechanisms to ensure the survival of the group, even if the mechanisms occasionally acted at the expense of the individual. This represents a critical juncture in the evolution of power: the combination of increased mental capacity and a need for group survival facilitated the evolution of culture as a mechanism to ensure the survival of the group's genetic code. Evolutionary adaptations that improved communication, planning and coordinated activity soon surfaced and increased the survivability of the group.

Evolutionary developments in the individual accompanied cultural evolution. Many of the features that evolved improved the ability of the group to control the individual, creating a positive feedback loop in the co-development of the gene and group culture. Better group control of the individual facilitated developments that strengthened the group's probability of survival, in turn improving the probability of survival for the individual's genes. The genetic development of more advanced emotions in individuals proved especially beneficial to the group.[1] Individuals experience feelings like loyalty, affection, territoriality, group identity, security in numbers, etc. These emotions simply act as power-relationships: methods developed in the genes to ensure group integrity and survival by control of neurochemicals. They directly resulted in the survival of the genetic lineage.

---

1.   For an analysis of the development of the human emotional set, see "Prometheus Rising" by R. A. Wilson.

Here, the gene is no longer dependent on the survival of a single individual—as long as the group survived, the gene prospered.

This group-entity, or culture, is in effect a meta-individual, and is subject to similar internal evolutionary structures as an individual human. Richard Dawkins suggests the name for a component building block in the structure of culture: the *meme*.[2] The meme is the cultural equivalent of the gene, but unlike the gene we cannot reduce the meme to a tangible particle. It exists only as a pattern of power-relationships—but it acts as one of the most powerful patterns in existence. As meme-based culture developed, especially in more advanced primates, it became more and more independent of the gene, eventually taking on a life of its own. The line between benefiting the gene and benefiting the cultural meme began to blur. Witness the development of the Selfish Meme!

Memes drove individuals to act just as genes could: for the benefit of the survival of the meme, even if the meme's survival came at the expense of the individual. Unlike the gene, however, the meme resides in the group as a whole. It more readily sacrifices a component individual in order to enhance the survivability of the group. Flocks of Seychelles Warblers provide an excellent example of memetic self-sacrifice. Some warblers who have failed as individuals to nest and reproduce will sacrifice an entire mating season acting as tender and assistant to the nest of another warbler in the group. In the process, they deny their own genetic instinct to procreate. Such adaptive altruism ensures propagation of the group's genetic—and memetic—code.[3] The warbler's self-sacrificing behavior exists only in some groups of the same species, suggesting the learned nature of the behavior, and therefore that it has cultural (memetic) roots, not those of a genetically coded instinct. This behavior exists because it improves the odds of group survival, along with both the genes and memes carried by that group. Sociobiologists David Sloan Wilson and Eliot Sober have demonstrated that this form of group, or multi-level selection translates directly to humans: "at the behavioral level, it is likely that much of what people have evolved to do is *for the benefit of the group*" (their emphasis).[4]

---

2. "The Selfish Gene", Richard Dawkins.
3. "The Triumph of Sociobiology" by John Alcock, pgs 196–197.
4. "Unto Others: The Evolution and Psychology of Unselfish Behavior" by Eliot Sober and David Wilson, pg 194.

Such powerful use of altruism to benefit group survival develops readily through the mechanics of the group meme, but would have had an exceedingly difficult time developing through the mechanics of the gene. Had a genetic mutation that predisposed an individual to self-sacrifice sprung up in a single warbler, it would decrease the probability of that individual surviving to propagate the gene. Memetic mutations, however, survive in a host group, not in a single individual, thus enabling memes to develop a strategy of altruism—sacrificing an individual for the good of the meme's group host. The flexibility of a group host opens a world of new possible strategies. Stratification and specialization of individuals provides one example of a far-reaching possibility validated by the demands of group survival. Biologically, the ability to create different types of cells for different purposes enabled the development of all higher-order life. Similarly, the memetic ability to create and control the stratification of individuals within a group facilitated the intensification and institutionalization of hierarchy and complex-culture. The meme's ability to deal with stratified structures led to the economic specialization of individuals within a group, making possible tremendous innovations in political and social structure. New memetic patterns, with access to such powerful adaptations, spread quickly.

Genes and memes initially enjoyed a symbiotic relationship. A change in either that improved a group's prospects benefited both parties. However, memes and genes operate in a fundamentally different manner from one another. While genes directly control the structure of an individual's neurochemistry, and through that the behavior of their host, memes have no direct means to control the individual. A meme, without hardwired access to biological mechanisms, cannot directly affect neurochemical release. Memes must instead operate by co-opting the biological control mechanisms of genes. Genetic functions have proven slow to adapt, providing predictable, stable platforms for the meme. The rapid adaptability and flexibility of the meme enabled it to evolve the ability to trigger genetic functions for its own purposes. This provided memes with the ability to indirectly control neurochemical levels. Simply invoke the required stimuli—genetically hardwired for recognition as an instinct or emotion—and presto: chemical influence over individual behavior.

As meme-complexes, or culture, became increasingly effective at improving the odds of group survival, our ancestors experienced parallel genetic developments facilitating the ever-greater influence of memes over the behavior of the individual. The development of language and reasoning among primates serves as an excellent example of the symbiotic evolution between gene and meme. Increasing intelligence and genetically determined capacity for language led to increasingly effective group coordination in procuring food, making decisions about defense, etc. Groups with the most effective coordination and decision-making had the greatest odds of survival and propagation, creating pressure to select individuals with superior capacity for those skills. Groups that provided internal selection pressures emphasizing the primacy of language skills and intellect prospered and out-competed other groups for territory and scarce resources. This process led to the continual increase of intellect, vocal communication and sociability among primates. The symbiotic development of meme and gene resulted in genetic functions specifically selected for their ability to work with cultural-memetic power-relationships.

Memes continually refined power-relationships over individuals to the point where they could kill-off individuals who negatively impacted group survivability. Howard Bloom described this power-relationship in his concept of the *Inner Judge*, the ability of the human brain to recognize certain sets of cultural stimuli as a signal to remove itself from the population.[5] The Inner Judge function causes the release of neurochemicals with effects ranging from depression to apoptosis—biologically initiated suicide. The extreme rate of suicide among the aboriginal populations of Australia, Oceania and North America shows one example of this Inner Judge at work, where a widespread sense of hopelessness or lack of purpose drives suicide rates to as much as 500 times greater than that of non-aboriginals.[6]

Early cooperation between genes and memes improved the probability of the survival of each. Genetic evolution, however, still progressed at a rate limited by reproductive age; in humans, a mutation had to wait years until its host reached sexual maturity to achieve propagation. Memetic evolution works far faster. Even in small, isolated groups memetic advances could develop in time-spans as short as a few days. As the rapid pace of memetic evolution increasingly facilitated the meme's ability to use genetic programs as tools to ensure its own survival, the gene gradually became slave to the meme. The advance of memetic control mechanisms pushed quickly past the era of the Selfish Gene to the era of Selfish Culture.

---

5.   *The Global Brain*, by Howard Bloom.
6.   See http://www.aic.gov.au/crc/reports/tatz/ch6.pdf for a report on aboriginal suicide from the Australian Institute of Criminology.

With genes and memes manipulating us, using neurochemical releases and emotional states to ensure their survival, we find ourselves faced with difficult, penetrating questions about our identity. What does it mean to experience a feeling if we can rationally understand that the emotion stems from nothing more than a chemical response evolved to ensure that we act as efficient hosts and vectors to genes and memes? What of our hopes and goals? Do these hopes truly belong to us, or do they serve as nothing more than effective strategies to propagate bits of cultural code? Would we still love our children if the resulting nurturing didn't increase the chance of our genes' survival? What of our egos versus the reality of genetic and memetic power-relationships: do we exist as nothing more than vectors for power-complexes? Do we have free will and an individual identity, or should we see our individuality as merely a construct of how our genes and memes use us to propagate themselves through the unconscious mechanism of natural selection? These represent difficult questions. The scope of their impact on our lives serves as an indication that we stand to uncover fundamental relationships governing our existence. At this point the ego and rational understanding come into direct conflict—will we retreat back to a comfortable but now conscious delusion, or continue this exploration?[7] Can our ego survive if it learns the form of its own inner workings? Inside the psychological maze of self-knowledge stands the unknown; the path out may lead to fulfillment or misery. We will come to appreciate the concept of blissful ignorance as we press our inquiry.

---

7.   R. A. Wilson, in *Cosmic Trigger*, explores in depth the concept of rationality in conflict with ego, epitomized by his concept (drawing from Kafka) of "Chapel Perilous", the maze of self-doubt, fear and revelation that tends to accompany the dissolution of the self-serving ego complex.

4

The Rise of Symbolic Thought

Symbolic thought—specifically the ability to invent new abstract representations and metaphors—most differentiates humans from other species. A symbol belongs to a subclass of memes—defined as an abstract representation of an object or force. The genetic advances that led to the human ability to work with symbols precipitated the development of language, writing and religion. Primates (and some other animals) have varying ability to recognize symbols. Gorillas, such as Koko[1], have even combined and applied existing symbols in simple ways. The ability to invent new symbols, to create new representations and connections, however, remains a uniquely human trait, as well as the greatest accomplishment of the symbiotic development of our genes and memes. Mastery of the symbol makes humans and human society unique.

With the mature ability to use and create symbols, an entirely new universe of complexity opened to the meme. Human ability to create and manipulate symbols led to a flowering of spoken language. While physical adaptations continued to participate in the development of language, providing a broader and more controlled ability to form sounds, language resulted from our mental mastery of symbols.[2] Complex languages proved enormously more effective for use in group coordination and decision-making than did simple verbal or gestural communication. The memetic complexes of small, proto-human groups quickly capitalized

---

1. Koko is a gorilla trained in American Sign Language by psychologist Dr. Francine Patterson. After 28 years of training, he is capable of using over 1000 signs and can recognize over 2000 spoken words. He does not, however, have the ability to form grammatically or syntactically correct sentences, create new symbols, or create new uses for existing symbols. This illustrates that his symbolic ability is constrained to recognition and repetition, not manipulation and creation.
2. *Origins of the Modern Mind*, by Merlin Donald.

on the potential of language, developing profound new possibilities for the use of symbols, thereby aiding in the development of complex culture.

This great leap in the ability to handle information via symbols permitted an entirely new means of information storage and transfer. Among early primates, information existed at the group level only temporarily. The group quickly lost any information not retained in the memory of each individual. Advancements in human language permitted information storage in memetic devices such as stories and fables—huge information structures that existed in a group's collective memory. This permitted the standardization of information ("That's not how that story goes..."), quick recall ("Remember the story of...") and facilitated more effective transmission from generation to generation. Stories conveyed complex sets of information: rules governing group behavior, interpretations of human psychology and justification of political structures. The fact that stories and fables remain so prevalent today demonstrates their proven evolutionary value.

Memes quickly expanded beyond the linguistic confines of their human host. Through symbols, memes could exist in many forms, often with great permanence and accuracy. Written language took flexible, constantly mutating oral stories and—often literally—set them in stone. In time, great libraries sprung up dedicated to maintaining a culture's memes. The calcification of memes did not stop with writing. Public architecture such as burial mounds, government buildings and religious sites often appear strongly infused with memetic meaning. Memes could also manifest in other visual media: ritual ceremony, clothing and art all effectively store and pass on a culture's memes.[3]

Memes represent useful tools for the storage of our cultural memories and standards. We must not, however, forget that memes do not serve humanity—rather, they use us for *their* propagation. Sweeping cultural features such as standards of behavior, roles in society and expected emotional responses represent tools *of the meme-complex*. They serve to mold humans into effective agents of the meme's survival. They do not serve to guarantee our health and happiness beyond what they require to ensure that we remain effective hosts. The meme acts as a self-serving agent of control.

---

3.   See the discussion of External Symbolic Storage in Merlin Donald's "Origins of the Modern Mind"

Surpassing language and writing, religion rapidly developed as the ultimate memetic control. With a developing capacity for rational thought, individuals gained the ability to weigh the utility of their decisions. This did not constitute independent thought, free from the control of genes and memes. Rather, it constituted an ability to make decisions with the awareness of their perceived long-term results. Animals have long been able to weigh choices subconsciously in order to maximize the release of desired neurochemicals for instant gratification. Rational thought allowed humans to attempt to consciously maximize their desired emotional or psychological states. Significantly, the *conscious* attempt to maximize these states worked most effectively over longer time frames, in complex cultural environments, and allowed the individual to consider the demands of the ego. Individuals could now act, believing that their actions represented a sacrifice today for greater happiness in the long run, e.g. making sacrifices today to ensure the well being of their offspring or the survival of the group. Happiness, of course, exists as no more than a genetically programmed desire for neurochemical release. This does not exclude the meme—the meme co-opts the entire complex of happiness into the larger sense of the ego, ensuring that memetic prosperity remains the end result of un-informed rationality. Ultimately, the process of 'rational' thought leads to ever-greater self-sacrifice in the name of the meme. This increasing drive towards self-sacrifice eventually confronts an individual's lifespan: it wouldn't seem rational for an individual to sacrifice until death, never to experience the envisioned rewards. Religion, an advanced memetic control mechanism, brought the promise of an after-life, making rational a complete lifetime of "self-sacrifice" to benefit the group's meme. An eternal afterlife in paradise loomed as the ultimate, rational reward. Under this logic, an individual could justify sacrificing their entire life to hard work, or to willingly die in combat. Throughout history, the promise of eternal bliss has functioned as a powerful motivator.

One can easily conceptualize the flow of power-relationships between genes and the individual, but the power-relationships between the individual and a meme seem more difficult to envision. Ultimately, however, both represent nothing more than mechanisms for controlling something else. They exist as collections of power-relationships, just as in the earlier example of an oxygen atom. They appear as much "real" as matter or energy. When viewed through the lens of power-relationships, there seems little difference between a complex of symbols and a complex of molecules.

Perhaps the most lasting contribution of symbolic thought remains the individual's ability to represent itself in symbol—conscious self-awareness, and ultimately the ego.[4] The conceptualization of the ego created a wide range of psychological errata, most significantly the sense of the sacred—or separate—status of humans from nature.[5] The self-aware separation of the individual, specifically the awareness that we exist for a limited time and then die, proved fertile ground for the development of spiritual and religious memes.

The ego also facilitated an entirely new basis for cultural stratification and organization. It served as the key that removed the last barrier to complete memetic control over humanity. The need for a meme to co-opt genetic mechanisms in order to control humans limited the reach and flexibility of cultural-memetic power-relationships. But with the increased ability of the human brain to process and store symbols, the individual now hosts memes that act entirely internally. The ego serves as a splice between these internal memes that co-opt genetic mechanisms and memes that link individuals with the larger cultural complex. It acts like a harness, providing a ready point of attachment for memes to control humans without the need to interface directly with genetically hard-wired responses. With new, and more capable channels of control, memes could motivate individuals to pursue more complex goals such as the accumulation of artifacts or the drive to acquire abstract power. Memes could even influence behavior through culturally encoded sets of abstract morals. The ego links such neuro-chemically-driven instinct to concepts of morality, aesthetics, family structure, changing gender roles and nearly every other memetic component of human society. Much of our psychological errata also stems from the practice of memes using primal genetic programs for other than their initially intended purpose.[6] This developing interface of symbols and neurochemicals paved the way for the next great leaps in human cultural complexity.

---

4. As a means of relating an individual's interaction with itself, and with genes and memes, I have used the concept of ego alone, rather than Freud's divisions of ego, id and superego, as my intent is to elucidate the nature of human interactions, not intra-actions.
5. *Traces of an Omnivore* by Paul Sheppard.
6. Jungian, Freudian and other schools of psychology essentially identify the side effects of imperfections in the interface between genes and memes.

5

Agriculture: Burning the Bridge to our Past

The advent of agriculture had a greater impact on humanity than any other event in our history. It created surpluses and intensifications leading to competition for limited resources and the formation of more complex social structures. It ended the genetic evolution of humanity as it existed for millions of years, and finally completed the transition of power over human action from the gene to the meme. It laid the foundation for what we recognize today as civilization. Agriculture, widely recognized as a great leap forward in human history, has in actuality done more than anything else to subjugate our daily lives to the control of a selfish culture.

Agriculture and the meme enjoyed a great period of symbiotic development. Evidence, however, demonstrates that symbolic memes preceded agriculture by thousands of years.[1] These did not appear, initially, as parallel developments—while agriculture led to the intensification of symbolic thought, the symbol first plowed the way for the farmer. Symbolic fluency permitted the development of structures within human society that proved essential to the

---

1. Fully developed symbolic manipulation and creation is at least as old as the cave paintings of Altamira, Spain. The charcoal pigment in the paintings has been radiocarbon dated to 12,000 years before present, +/- 400 years (Nature magazine, issue 68, pgs 68–70). However, recent findings suggest that the Aterian groups of Northern Africa utilized art and symbolic processes as long as 90,000 years ago (see "What is Aterian" by Maxine Kleindienst in "Oasis Papers: Proceedings of the First International Symposium of the Dahkleh Oasis Project", 2001). The earliest confirmed agricultural community, the settlement of Catal Huyuk, in modern-day Turkey, dates back possibly as far as 11,000 years before present (exact dating, specifically confirming the city's use of agriculture, still requires refinement. See "Bayesian Statistics and the Dating of Çatalhöyük East" by C. Cessford, 2002).

19

adoption and intensification of agriculture. One such structure, the abstract concept of land ownership, proved manageable through symbolic representation of territory. One cannot literally pick up land and exchange it, but one can represent land symbolically—in the form of a deed, for example. As long as all parties accept the symbolic representation of land, then it becomes possible to own, exchange or sell the symbol. The process of intensification—the catalyst for all future economic, political and cultural evolution—began with the meme's ability to incorporate this concept of ownership into its complex of power-relationships.

The process of intensification, from an anthropologist's viewpoint, defines agricultural societies.[2] Intensification is the process through which self-replicating structures become increasingly more complex, interconnected and hierarchal. Intensification forms a positive feedback loop in the competition for one or more resources critical to the survival of a society. If several competing groups all strive to achieve competitive advantage through intensification, then they must each attempt to intensify faster than the other. Agricultural societies entered into inevitable conflict over limited resources because their means of production required the power to the exclusive use of a limited amount of arable land. Conflicts over land use supported further intensification as larger populations and greater surpluses acted as an evolutionarily successful means to victory. The competition for limited resources among several intensifying competitors caused an increase in the pace of intensification. Those cultures that intensified faster, that developed better means to control larger populations, out-competed their simpler rivals. Intensification demanded parallel improvements in both agricultural methods and political and economic structures—the efforts of ever-larger groups of agriculturalists required efficient management and direction. The concept of ownership played the critical role of connecting agricultural efficiency with political organization: power to control access to arable land translated to power to control societies dependent on the products of that land.

Agriculture did one thing that no previous complex of memes could: it trapped the population into continuing the present mode of production.[3] Agriculture controlled the individual by regulating access to the food supply. Individuals need food to live, and now, with agriculture and land-ownership, they needed

---

2.   For an excellent treatment of the role of intensification in the development of human society, see "On the Road of the Winds" by Patrick Kirch or "Bronze Age Economics" by Timothy Earle.

3.   "Beyond Civilization" Daniel Quinn.

[Handwritten margin notes: "Growth is a must for successful power pursuit — where power is the goal there must be growth"; "That would be improved by fewer people"; "never ending"; "Agriculture → needed for..."; "GROWTH"; "who control food — controls people"; "Agriculture didn't cause the Fall, just made it inevitable."]

their culture to get food. In the preceding hunter-gatherer economic mode all but the very young or infirm had open access to food, no strings attached. With agriculture, due to the need to access farming land (controlled by the cultural power structure) to get food, the individual became indentured to the local cultural power-complex. After a few generations, individuals in primarily agricultural systems had lost the knowledge (the power) to return to the hunter-gatherer mode. Even more decisively, the increase in population facilitated by agriculture made a return of large portions of the population to hunting and gathering impossible.[4] Such a population density required the use of agriculture. The culture now controlled the food, and therefore the individual. This no longer represented a power-relationship of highly suggestive neurochemical influences. This relationship demanded compliance or starvation.

Additionally, agriculture virtually ended biological evolution for humans. There remain a few, very minor exceptions, such as the improved lactose tolerance of Northern Europeans that probably developed alongside pastoralism and agriculture, but evolution in general has switched from individual selection to group selection. While, in agricultural societies, some individuals would not live to reproduce, this resulted increasingly less often from lower individual fitness. Instead, if the group prospered, far more members survived, regardless of individual fitness. With the end of biological evolution, the makeup of our genome froze in the Pleistocene era of hunter-gatherers.[5] Cultural evolution remained the only game in town, but it still relied on a human host. The need for rapidly advancing culture to remain compatible with a structure frozen in the time of hunter-gatherers will prove a defining theme when we consider our present situation in Chapter VIII.

With the end of human evolution based on natural selection, evidence continues to surface that the development of humanity seems to follow ever closer to the path of selective breeding. In modern, industrial society, humans tend to choose partners of similar intellectual capability, providing a selection mechanism to 'breed' our species into ever more divergent groups. This frightening theory sug-

---

4.   There is some evidence of hierarchal civilizations being abandoned and their populations returning to tribal hunting and gathering, specifically the Olmec civilization of Mesoamerica. See "Beyond Civilization" by Daniel Quinn.

5.   The Pleistocene era runs from 1.8 million to 11,000 years ago. It comprised the critical stage in the genetic development of humanity culminating in Homo Sapiens Sapiens, our current form.

gests that culturally applied influence in the selection of mates may force humanity to diverge into multiple species, providing economic stratification of the workforce. Like the Eloi and Morlocks of H. G. Wells' "Time Machine", or the division of bees in a hive, one human species could specialize as the droning laborers and another as the organizer, innovator and leader. Stratification of the species may also prove evolutionarily viable as it could provide specialized hosts capable of accommodating even more demanding memes. For example, a caste of bred laborers may develop an increased ability to tolerate memes that demand increasingly mechanized and monotonous daily routines, without the side effects of depression or rebellion. Such an extreme scenario could manifest in a relatively short time, as breeding can produce new species orders of magnitude faster than classical evolution.

Agriculture represents one of the seminal developments in human history. Its two primary impacts—the end of human biological evolution and the enslavement of the agriculturalist to his culture—have influenced all subsequent events. Agriculture set the stage for the rise of culture, for the meme to dominate the gene. We will see the effects of memetic domination in our exploration of the development of economics, politics and technology.

Addiction to MORE

Growth of a cancer that is not part of symbiotic whole and playing by common rules but has its own self-serving rules and is committed to growth continuous

6

Economics: The Anthropology of Freedom

wanting people to have more

Until now we have considered the two distinct nexuses of power-relationships within our lives: the gene and the meme. While genetic evolution takes place over a time span of millions of years, the pace of cultural evolution has quickened exponentially with intensification. Development of new memes that may have taken a full generation in the Pleistocene can now transpire in a year, a day or less. The increased scope and interconnectivity of our culture has resulted in amazing developments in memetic structures. In particular, memetic advancement has made possible two remarkable cultural constructs: the marketplace and the state. Through these institutions human society transitioned from simple tribes to global empires. *civilization*

The market acts as a memetic entity that processes information, connecting capability and desire. It has the ability to organize other meme-driven collections of human activity by connecting the possible outputs and desired inputs of each with a complementary match. The marketplace has evolved from inter-group feasts exchanging surpluses and specialties through an elaborate series of gifts[1] to computer-mediated exchanges using price to regulate the global production, transportation and consumption of countless commodities.

The state emerges as a closely related development, often inseparable from the market. The gradual intensification of inter-personal power-relationships and the growth of cultural institutions directing human action stemmed from an increasing scarcity of environmental resources. As populations grew and environmental

growing population

1. For an excellent examination of the process of competitive inter-group feasting, or potlaching, as a catalyst to social organization, see "Economic Man", by Harold Schneider, 1974.

constraints exerted selection pressures on competing groups, those with the greater ability to harness resources and direct populations survived and prospered. More advanced markets—critical to success in economic competition—flourished in the stable, ordered environment of the increasingly hierarchal state. The state created an environment capable of supporting memetic structures such as a code of laws and a representative currency that greatly improved the efficiency of the market. The market and the state quickly grew into a tightly co-dependent pair.

The market-state complex developed from a fairly stable base: the hunter-gatherer tribe. Economically, the Domestic Mode of Production and Share-Out redistribution characterize the tribal form of organization.[2] In the Domestic Mode of Production, the household unit pools all production of staple goods for household use as needed. Items such as meat, tubers, tools, shelter and clothing exist as products of the household, freely distributed to its members. This creates little pressure towards intensification of political or economic structures as the aggregate demand remains carefully balanced with the supply capacity of each household, and institutionalized exchange does not occur. Similarly, Share-Out served as the predominant method of redistribution—equally distributing the product of cooperation among the participants. In the example of the cooperative hunt, while only one individual may have killed an animal, the meat was shared among the participants in the hunt, affecting redistribution throughout the tribe. Such egalitarian economies incorporated equally egalitarian political structures. Tribes (not the same as chiefdoms[3]) utilized voluntary participation and group discussion to maintain order. Remnant tribes today continue to exhibit strong cultural aversion towards status or rank of any type.[4]

Egalitarian structure provided continuity in the evolution to Homo Sapiens Sapiens,[5] with remarkably stable, tribal organization spanning thousands of generations of human evolution. What catalyzed the development of more complex state and market structures from the tribal form of organization? The answer to

2.   "Stone Age Economics", Marshal Sahlins, 1972
3.   Timothy Earle, in "Bronze Age Economics" provides labels for the progressively more centralized and hierarchal forms of human society: Tribe, Big-Man Group, Chiefdom, Proto-State and State.
4.   Hunters in the Dobe Ju/'hoansi tribe will insult the quality or size of their catch, so that they are seen as modest, and not superior to the hunters who have failed to return with a kill. See "The Dobe Ju/'hoansi" by Richard B. Lee, 1993.

this puzzle may lie in the observation that, in most ecosystems, the hunter-gatherer mode of production only functions at low population densities (anywhere from 1/10th to 1/100th that of primitive agricultural civilizations[6]). Gradually, memetic mutation led scattered groups to experiment with agricultural techniques such as encouraging the growth of favored foraging foods (often by burning older growth to clear the way for certain fauna), small scale planting, etc. Differing evidence suggests that the adoption of the related phenomenon of pastoralism may have resulted, not from purely random mutation, but from conscious transition in the face of specific climate change events. One such example appears in the Dahkleh Oasis, in the Western Desert of Egypt. Here, semi-sedentary hunter-gatherer populations flourished for several hundred thousand years.[7] Then, 10,000 years ago, the Pleistocene savannah of North Africa transitioned to the Holocene Sahara Desert that exists today. The Dahkleh Oasis shifted from the fertile center of a vast, habitable region to a virtual island in a sea of nearly lifeless sand. Archaeological evidence[8] suggests that as the Dahkleh population retreated into an increasingly constrained oasis, they experimented with taming and domesticating a wide variety of animals—probably even giraffe. Eventually, it seems likely that cattle-based pastoralism dominated their economy, as cattle represented a mobile and long-lived food bank well suited to the Dahkleh's unique environmental challenges. Here, climate change acts as a catalyst for this transition, overcoming the attraction of the superior efficiency and suitability to the human genome of the hunting and gathering mode of production. This link may provide some hint as to why agriculture and pastoralism appeared independently, and nearly simultaneously, at many locations around the world: the climate change that appears to have affected the Dahkleh Oasis 10,000 years ago also affected the entire planet, representing the end of the last Ice Age.

Most groups, when not forced by environmental influences, quickly abandoned their experimentation with agriculture. But in some cases—especially, it appears,

5. *Homo Sapiens Sapiens* is the name of the current human subspecies. Dating from at least 130,000 B.C.E. (the date of the earliest reconstructed skull of our subspecies). Often called "The Symbol User", the name translates literally to "wise, wise"—something that may prove ironic if we are not able to overcome the issues addressed later in this book.

6. "Guns, Germs and Steel", Jared Diamond, 1997.

7. "Mixed Memoirs", Gertrude Caton-Thompson, 1983.

8. "Secrets of the Sand: Revelations of Egypt's Everlasting Oasis", Harry Thurston, pgs. 72–119, 2003.

These were they grew for power maximized

in the face of environmental catalysts—experimentation led to population growth, or at least stability. When coupled with similar experimentation and population growth by neighboring groups, competition for agricultural land and resources provided pressure to select for the continuation and intensification of agriculture. Agriculture, including incipient agriculture, did not convert hunter-gatherers with the promise of a better quality of life—in fact, agriculture provided just the opposite. Statistically, agriculturalists work longer hours and have poorer nutrition than hunter-gatherers.[9] Why, then, did much of humanity adopt agricultural practices? Population pressure among hunter-gatherers does not appear to answer the question, as "populations didn't significantly increase until agriculture was instituted."[10] Instead, it appears that some groups who experimented with the powerful technology of agriculture got swept away in a vicious cycle of intensification. As neighbors began to compete for limited resources, scarcity provided the evolutionary pressure to select for intensified economic and political processes.[11]

growth, power maximization

This vicious cycle of incipient agriculture appears to have occurred independently, and roughly simultaneously, at several locations around the globe. All of these locations combined higher-density hunter-gatherer populations, fauna suitable to agricultural development along with the catalyst of climate change. Tribes had understood the principles of agriculture for at least 6,000 years before the first agricultural civilization[12], but chose to continue the hunter-gatherer mode of production because it represented a more efficient means of meeting subsistence needs.[13] While tribes that experimented with agriculture experienced a net loss of productivity, they gained the ability to support far denser populations on a given area of land. Population growth, however, continued even after the population reached the local carrying capacity for incipient agriculture, resulting in expansionary pressures. As neighboring agriculturalists began to compete for arable land, those tribes that further intensified through methods such as irrigation gained a greater advantage in the form of a larger population of warriors. The ability to harness the power of greater production, coordinating the action of larger populations in a manner that provided a competitive advantage, also

Pushed by those in power

---

9.   "The Original Affluent Society", Marshal Sahlins, in "Stone Age Economics".
10. John Zerzan, personal correspondence, 29 April, 2004.
11. "On the Road of the Winds", Patrick V. Kirch, 2000.
12. "Traces of an Omnivore", Paul Shepard, pg 181.
13. See the essay "The Original Affluent Society" in Marshal Sahlins' "Stone Age Economics".

check

To understand the process, we must first understand and accept what our civilization is!

required increased centralized decision-making. Tribal organization could not process the information needed to direct a large group. As tribes proved inadequate to handle such problems as mobilizing populations for large irrigation projects or coordinating larger-scale warfare, those groups that chanced upon more centralized control reaped the evolutionary advantage.

The transition seems to have led tribes to organize around "Big Men", sparking the formation of a centralized political control structure.[14] Stemming from the Share-Out concept of redistribution, those individuals who consistently provided greater harvests or catches would gain prestige by sharing with more needy group members in difficult times. The process of sharing surpluses eventually led individuals to join the production efforts of a single Big Man to both gain from their prestige and share in their success (superior management skill) in harvest. The centralized direction of the Big Man allowed for organized wars of conquest, the construction of large-scale irrigation projects, etc. Scarcity and selection pressures favored those Big Men that created the most intensified, centralized structure. This process resulted not entirely from random events and evolutionary pressures. Big Men often rose to their position as the result of exceptional organizational skills, so to some degree one can view this intensification, the "attempt to mobilize resources to finance institutions, as a conscious strategy."[15] The intensification of the relationship between centralized director and contributor, along with the resulting stratification of individuals within a group, prompted the transition from tribe to state.

In the process of intensification the individual steadily lost power and control. In contrast to the freely available resources of the hunter-gatherer world, scarcity and agriculture demanded that an individual remain a member of the group in order to maintain access to arable land and hunting grounds. Resources that the incipient state defended, the state also owned. Gaining access to them meant accepting the demands of the state, accepting the power relationship of the state over the individual. Forced acceptance of hierarchy formed a positive feedback loop, paving the way towards ever more complex and controlling forms of political and economic systems.

Hierarchy—the stratification of individuals to provide efficient command and control of specialized individual and group functions—became the key trait link-

---

14. *Bronze Age Economics*, Timothy Earle.
15. Timothy Earle, personal correspondence, 17 September, 2003.

ing the Market and the State. An example of an evolutionarily successful pattern, hierarchy met the demands of intensification across a diverse set of cultural considerations. This does not simply demonstrate a case of hierarchal political organization succeeding. Rather it serves as a case of hierarchy as a successful, self-replicating pattern applied across economic, political and social structures. The Marketplace and the State evolved together through intensification and the application of the pattern of hierarchy, continuing the trend toward increasing intensification and organization of human activity. Cultural memetic complexes enabled the process. Not only did they pave the way for the acceptance of hierarchy, they also evolved to serve the critical function of buffering the increasing demands placed on individuals with the tolerances of the human genome. What many think of as distinct political, economic and cultural processes in today's world continue to progress towards ever more interconnected meta-networks of power-relationships. Market and State combined, buffered by cultural mechanisms, began to form unified memetic superstructures. This powerful combination continued to intensify, gradually joined by the intensification of another family of memes: technology.

7

Neutral Technology and the Demands of Power

interesting. we adopt a new technology to help us but it may totally unexpected outcomes produce

The old saying that "knowledge is power" appears more correct than many realize. Technology breaks down to, literally, knowledge of techniques and processes. We must not consider knowledge itself as alive, not possessing the anthropomorphic qualities of good or evil. But the application, the animation of technology, creates power-relationships internal and external to its users. Returning to agriculture, we have a clear example of a technology's power-relationships placing demands on the users of a technology that often become unobserved and non-voluntary. Agriculturalists must employ certain symbolic constructs, entirely new power-relationships, in their employment of the *technic-knowledge* of agriculture.[1] These new power-relationships represent the hidden demands of technology. Agriculture required ownership, sedentary populations, hierarchal government and social stratification to create and defend production structures. Critically, agriculture supported population densities that required the continuation of agriculture. People in most environments simply could not abandon agriculture. Most ecosystems could support only dramatically lower population densities should their populations revert back to a hunter-gatherer mode of production. So, while we should not define the technology of agriculture as inherently "evil", like all technologies it has had powerful, unanticipated and often irreversible effects on its users.

The case of the *artisan versus the assembly line* provides a similar example of technic-knowledge. The artisan, an individual who crafts a product through the entire chain of events needed to add value for an outside user, has the complete

---

1. Knowledge of technics—processes and methods—forms the technology of Agriculture. Jaques Ellul provides an excellent treatment of technology in *The Technological Society*.

Technology, indeed, may have irreversible effect on humanity.

set of knowledge needed to perform the transformation. For example, the watchmaker transforms metal through a variety of phases until it has reached the stage of a finished watch. Similarly the potter makes clay into finished pottery, the carpenter makes trees into furniture, etc. Each has the power to transform a material into a value-added product. Opposite the artisan stands the case of the assembly line. In the assembly line, individuals perform highly specialized segments of the value-adding process, but none have the knowledge to affect the full transformation. The use of the technology of specialization provides more efficient production, from the perspective of the capitalist, but a loss of power for the individual. Instead of the individual artisan, the *assembly line* holds the power over its human components. The production knowledge exists embedded in the process and outside of the control of the individual. The assembly line serves as an example of technology in control of people.

Can we consider neutral a technology that exists outside the control of its users, and that exerts upon them considerable influence? We should not view such technologies as sentient, conscious entities that desire to inflict harm on their human "users". A lumber company that clear-cuts forests to sustain its profits and ensure its survival does not specifically intend, for the sake of "evil", to inflict destruction on nature. Yet we cannot consider it neutral. The common argument for the unquestioning acceptance of technology remains this: *technology does not have a good or evil nature. Rather, it has a neutral nature, which humans can use for good or bad.* This statement has a clear flaw—it presupposes that humanity exerts control over the technologies it uses, not the other way around. As we have seen, we do not control the power centers of the gene, the meme or market—rather they use us as vectors for their survival. Humans must not define technology as neutral if it does not exist entirely under their control. While they do not exhibit conscious intention, technologies follow a hard-wired path of all self-replicating entities: *selfish interest.* Any entity that does not pursue its own self-interest in an environment of competition quickly ceases to exist. Technologies and other power-relationship complexes that have become widely employed by humans generally pass the test of evolutionary fitness. In other words, they survive because they function in a method that ensures their continuation. Like a virus, technology's survival depends on the manipulation of human societies to serve as hosts and vectors. Also like a virus, long-term survival depends on ensuring the survival of the host population. We must use caution not to mistake the unconsciously selfish memes that we call technology with harmless or neutral tools for human use.

may enable evil and use it

of course new technology

with the evil freed, MD will always take advantage of it for its own selfish advantage

In an environment rich in meme-complexes competing for limited resources, the evolutionary advantage favors the entity that tends to intensify. If, in the process of intensification, plants or animals overshoot the carrying capacity of their environment then they must die back to a sustainable level. The human population acts as the host environment for the family of meme-complexes, with humans in turn depending on their hosts, the physical environment. With the increasing connectivity and scope of human interaction, the meme complex has become the Selfish-Intensifying Meme. The pace of intensification continues to accelerate, with unforeseeable results for the human hosts. Perhaps the direst of the possible consequences remains that the intensity and complexity of a meme-complex may push its human hosts to overshoot the carrying capacity of the entire Earth, resulting in the same dieback encountered in the study of ecosystems.[2] Many skeptics point out that we have no reason to doubt our capability to develop sufficient new technologies to accommodate an ever-increasing population, as we always have in the past. This logic runs into the brick wall of the realities of geometric growth; as an extreme example, at some point the sheer weight of human biomass will outweigh the Earth itself. It is axiomatic that perpetual growth, like perpetual motion, represents an impossibility. Oddly, those who express skepticism about this concept often consist of the same people who point out the benefits of investments compounding over time—as economist Kenneth Boulding said, "anyone who believes exponential growth can go on forever is either a madman or an economist."[3]

Misplaced faith in perpetual growth exists as a by-product of the intensifying, hierarchal master pattern that underlies most aspects of human society. Despite the clear reality that we live within a system limited by finite resources, our entire economy rests on the need for continual growth.

The publicly owned corporation serves as an example of a pervasive pattern that cannot accept stability; if it does not provide a regular, growth-based return to its investors, it will find itself quickly dissolved. The press, politicians and the general public often rush to express surprise at the corporate decision making process. Why won't corporations act as more responsible citizens, help protect the

---

2. See http://www.dieoff.org for an excellent discussion of human population projections and their impact on our survival.

3. Kenneth Boulding, former president of the American Economics Association, author of *Economic Analysis*, as quoted in *Adbusters* Volume 12 Number 5 (September/October 2004).

environment, or take better care of their employees? Doing so may provide long-term benefits, not only for society, but also for the corporation's bottom line. Ultimately, however, the very structure of the corporation constrains it in its decision making process: it must respond to the short-term demand to increase shareholder value, resulting in the ubiquitous, shortsighted decision making of corporate America. Like the corporation, economists see serious trouble for a country's economy as a whole if it *temporarily stops growing*,[4] as the debt and inflation based finance structure cannot handle *mere stability*. Any entity, whether a small business or a national economy, that finances its operation by borrowing money at interest *must continually grow* in order to remain solvent due to the demands of repaying the time-value of money. No wonder, then, that with an institutionalized demand for continuous growth, our society seems willing to ignore the clear realities of finite resources. This process begs the question: should we view environmental overshoot as a possibility or as a foregone conclusion if we continue with our present economic structure?

We can observe examples of technological memes pushing humanity towards possible environmental overshoot in the industrial revolution, mass production and specialization. Not only have these new processes continued intensification, further increasing our dependence on them for our survival, they also place broad demands on their human hosts. While I will demonstrate why economic specialization and hierarchal organization create their own systemic problems, they do generate initial gains in production efficiency. The problem remains that production must remain compatible with the human host—a host genetically optimized for a late-Pleistocene, hunter-gatherer existence. Intensified specialization of production results in a highly stratified work force, often demanding mind-numbingly routine individual functions, and requires a level of human interaction and organization that seems increasingly incompatible with our genetically optimum small-tribe environment. The high-profile emergence of Attention Deficit Hyperactivity Disorder provides one example of human incompatibility with the demands of the industrial economy. Researchers have demonstrated that this "disorder" acts as an evolutionarily beneficial development of hunter-gather society, but that it remains medically suppressed because it makes workers incompatible with the demands of the modern economy.[5] The economic meme-complex succeeds in ensuring that we remain superficially compatible with an environ-

---

4.   One common definition of recession: when the economy does not demonstrate positive growth in GDP for two consecutive quarters.

5.   "Whose Order is Being Disordered by ADHD", Thom Hartmann.

f everyone trien to give up on
ur civilization, it will not allow it.
So, this is all or nothing. Individually
we may try

ment in which we increasingly represent just a cog in the works. Stopgap measures ensure human compatibility with this system, but they often prove antithetical to human health and happiness: examples include our increasing drug dependencies, medicated suppression of Bloom's "Inner Judge" of depression, television hypnosis and vicariously living our unfulfilled dreams through the surrogate of an increasingly integrated media complex. The tendency to accept conditions that do not appear compatible with our genome serves as an evolutionary adaptation in its own right: cultures most capable of placating their hosts, while intensifying faster-than-ever, prove more evolutionarily viable. They tend to absorb or destroy competing cultures that have sacrificed intensification for human happiness. *That's true. And scary.*

winners again?

Cultures that fail to develop, that resist or rebel against the continual intensification of production, have historically been unable to keep up with their intensifying neighbors. We can see their failure today in the rampant destruction of primitive and folk-culture around the world by American-style mass-media consumerism. Domination by more centralized, intensified cultures has been a theme throughout history, from the chiefdoms of Polynesia to the emergence of unified empires in ancient China. We would likely have more concern for the trend if our oblivious acceptance of the droning pace and pain of *progress* did not exist as another trait selected for in the global evolution of culture.

The current debate on globalization epitomizes the epic struggle of intensifying cultural meme-complexes facing off against the boundaries of human tolerance. Globalization—the dramatic, worldwide intensification and integration of meme-complexes—has steadily accelerated since World War II. Taking advantage of a revolution in communication technology, modern markets developed the ability to connect separate and highly specialized production and demand more efficiently than ever. This results in the creation of an integrated, memetic super-structure that transcends every aspect of human interaction.

And this true, control is through markets

From an economic standpoint, globalization finally succeeds in reducing the human component in production to a mere commodity, unconcerned with place, ready for optimization just like any other supply chain or production line. Spurred on by the nearly limitless mobility of capital and the increasing affordability of global transportation,[6] we take raw materials from all corners of the globe—increasingly from locations with low labor costs and lax environmental regulations. We then ship these materials around the world for manufacture into consumer products in an appropriately sweatshop-friendly locale, finally offering them for sale to consumers worldwide. The competition to attract increasingly marginal jobs by marketing lower labor costs and fewer environmental restrictions to globe-hopping corporations represents but one result of such extreme mobility of capital and products.[7]

Economists seek to steer our economies toward the optimization of a known goal. Goals such as human health, happiness and security may seem obvious to some, but in reality the goal seems institutionally fixed. The process of evolution within a system dominated by competing hierarchies demands that one set of goals consume all others: continuous growth, expansion, and increased domination. Any corporation or nation that pursues a more human-oriented goal will soon find itself squeezed out of existence for not following the simple rules of natural selection. We can only maintain such continuous growth through the perpetual increase in demand for products and the increased efficiency of supplying those products. Globalization results in the institutionalization of continuous growth, forcing production of a given product to the most efficient possible place and scale. Since the input to production provided by human labor and intellect exists as nothing more than another factor for optimization, we will soon trim away any expenses dedicated to improving individual health, happiness or security beyond the bare minimum. If such expenses don't improve production efficiency, then they do not support the unstated economic goal of continuous growth.

Globalization appears fundamentally similar to the intensifications of the agricultural and industrial revolutions, but an order of magnitude greater in its speed and scope. Likewise, it requires ever more elaborate mechanisms to placate the human component, keeping the demands nominally within our genetic tolerance. If we do not find a way to reverse the trend, the most pertinent question may be: which tolerance will we reach first, that of human ontogeny or of the global environment?

---

6.   Phenomena largely due to subsidization. Hierarchy's key tools in dealing with its internal inefficiencies (discussed further in Chapter IX) leverage its centralization of power to subsidize the key mechanisms of continuing intensification. This manifests today in the intense subsidy of fossil fuel use, car-culture and easily available, government-backed loans.

7.   For an excellent discussion of Globalization and the impact of capital mobility on labor, see Michael Shuman's "Going Local".

Scientists and economists have proposed many models to bring economics and human ontogeny back into harmony. Some tout the virtues of localization and community currency as tools to combat globalization.[8] Lester R. Brown of the Earth Policy Institute suggests solving the problem by modifying accounting standards to include future environmental damage as a realized cost.[9] Others have suggested that statistical changes, such as using median instead of mean per capita income, would rectify the problem—the Kingdom of Bhutan has even adopted Gross National Happiness as their policy benchmark. One thing is clear: humanity has never suffered from a shortage of ideas, and yet none have managed to end the dominance of the hierarchal pattern of power organization. To do that—to affect true change—we must first learn to control ourselves, and then learn to control the very fabric of power itself.

---

8.   "Going Local", Michael Schuman.
9.   "Eco-Economy: Building an Economy for the Earth", Lester R. Brown, 2001.

8

Self-Aware: Ego and Power

[handwritten marginalia: Mother Culture / Power . we are slave to our genes but not to memes]

Consider the question first presented in Chapter III: what will become of our individuality, our egos as we gain awareness of the underlying genetic and memetic power-relationships? Do we consist of more than just vectors for power-complexes? Do we have free will and an individual identity, or do we exist as nothing more than a construct of how our genes and memes use us to propagate? Can we resolve the conflict between rationality and ego?

Susan Blackmore, in her book *The Meme Machine*, advocates acquiescence to our fate as the subjects of our culture.[1] But as already mentioned, our culture, left unrestrained, will ultimately breach the limitations of either humanity or the environment. We should reject such an approach as it leads to the end of humanity, the end of life on Earth, or both. Technology, too, threatens the very essence of humanity. Genetic engineering and nanotechnology may well shift consciousness from the individual to the group, eliminating the very essence of the individual. Francis Fukuyama warns of just such a possibility, but states that "[we] do not have to regard ourselves as slaves to inevitable technological progress when that progress does not serve human ends."[2] A way forward exists, a path that will lead us to a sane and satisfying relationship with each other, with the Earth and with power. Such a path requires that we first gain a firm understanding of two concepts—*who we "are"*, and what vision *we want* to work towards.

What we "are", what we can best represent ourselves as—the vectors of genes and memes—saw explanation in previous chapters. The difficult question that we must now resolve remains *how do we best define the nature of our identity?* Does our sense of self—our ego—exist as anything more than an illusion serving the same masters as our bodies? Can we ever identify the true core to ourselves, not

---

1. "The Meme Machine", Susan Blackmore.
2. "Our Posthuman Future", Francis Fukuyama, pg 218.

just an illusory construct of evolution? Ultimately there remains one inescapable realization: a core of individuality does not exist. We "are" assemblages constructed as tools to benefit entities external to the ego-illusion. As in Plato's allegory of the cave, our entire paradigm, our sense of self, remains predicated upon the shadows that memes cast on the wall of our consciousness.[3] The honest realization of our nature comes from the confrontation of our perceptions of self and ego. Countless religious, societal and psychological constructs exist to deny or cope with the problems of ego, but the key to escaping delusional constructs lies in acceptance of the ego-illusion. This realization acts as the gateway to enlightenment in the world's greatest mystical traditions.

Beyond the illusion of ego exists a deeper conceptualization of self: the universe consists of a swirling, dynamic dance of power-relationships, with the black-and-white construct of the individual giving way to the grayer concept of the individual as a nexus of these connections. No true separation between individual and environment remains. Our consciousness has developed as a tool used by other entities, but it has provided the ultimate tool *for our use* to which no other nexus has access: self-awareness. The understanding that self-awareness exists to serve the meme *breaks that bond of servitude*—it acts as the realization of enlightenment. Re-read the last sentence. The individual re-emerges as a discrete point of true awareness—not delusional ego-awareness, but awareness of our status as a nexus in the dance of power-relationships. Every atom in our body changes, replaced with new matter through the course of eating, metabolism and elimination—we literally do not consist of the same substance today that we did last year. At death we remain physically the same structure, but not the same entity. These examples illustrate that we exist as much more than a complex assemblage of particles. Our true substance seems to more closely resemble a hub and relay to vast webs of power-relationships. While we exist in a constant state of physical flux, we remain a stable, self-aware nexus. Coming to terms with our existence merges science and spirituality, leading ultimately down the classical path of enlightenment-beyond-ego. This realization will set us free.

---

3.   Plato's allegory of the cave: prisoners are seated in a cave, heads chained such that they can only look at one wall. From behind them, a fire casts light on that wall. Puppeteers use objects to create shadows on the wall. Plato's point is that the shadows on the wall represent full reality to the prisoners, but the outside observer can easily observe that the shadows "are" not reality—just like the case of the ego illusion and the meme.

well, not necessary. Just small groups, proper food physical movement — such things that we need to rec

Part of the acceptance of our self as a self-aware nexus in a dynamic world remains the acceptance of our genetic ontogeny.[4] We exist, genetically, as organisms optimized to operate in the late Pleistocene era of small hunter-gatherer tribes. Our physical and psychological systems evolved to function optimally under increasingly different conditions from those encountered in the globalizing, industrial world. Any world we wish to create must then act compatibly with the requirements of our genome. As we gain a better understanding of the requirements of our genes, and how they exert control over us, we will have better ability to take conscious control of those mechanisms. Addiction, depression, fear and anxiety can all come under control through our understanding of their neurochemical mechanisms, and why these reactions initially evolved.[5] For example, understanding the triggers and functions of our body's sympathetic and parasympathetic responses permits—with practice—increased control of these functions.[6] Meditation and breathing exercises, cornerstones of many esoteric traditions, essentially provide means to gain control of some of our body's autonomic systems. With further research and careful application, there exists the potential to take conscious control of our genetic programming.

Exactly — just different

Creating a world that provides compatibility with our genes will ultimately require addressing how memes control us. Gaining conscious control of genetically programmed responses prevents memes from co-opting those responses without our permission. By breaking the meme's control over our wants, needs

Now we are talking.

---

4. Our genetic ontogeny—the course of humanity's evolution in the setting of small, hunter-gatherer tribes—is what most defines us. Paul Shepard, in "Traces of an Omnivore", explores the concept and its conflict with our modern lives in great depth.

5. For most of us, our formal education never gave us the owner's guide to our body-mind that we deserve. See "Prometheus Rising" and "Quantum Psychology" by R. A. Wilson, "Mind Wide Open" by Steven Johnson, "The Strucutre of Magic" by Richard Bandler and John Grinder and "The Secret Teachings of All Ages" by Manly P. Hall.

6. Conscious breathing, in particular, seems to be a pathway to control over the body's sympathetic and parasympathetic responses. Try this simple exercise. Repeat the following four times: breathe in through the nose to the count of four, hold your breath to the count of seven, exhale through pursed lips to the count of eight. After the fourth time, immediately breathe in and out through the nose as quickly as possible for fifteen seconds. Then repeat the initial four breaths. Do this to obtain a relaxed, alert state of mind at a time when you find your body slipping unwillingly into "fight-or-flight" mode. See Andrew Weil's "Breathing" for additional information.

I don't buy it. That doesn't
come naturally
to us.

and actions, we can make choices and act to build a world that provides compatibility with our genome. We can begin to consciously shape memes, to create a set
of stable cultural-complexes that concentrate power in the hands of the individual, providing humans with great freedom and control over our environment.

we better learn to
leave in agreement
rather then control -

comply with natural laws
that govern our existence as
a species in our environ-
- ment

) Advocating for control
of what is unnatural just
digs us deeper into the
whole. This is not about
more control to deal with
the side system. It is about
surrendering our control to
the ultimate force that
govern our lives.

Forward, to Rhizome

The path to stability and sustainability in human society lies in the conscious manipulation of memetic control structures. Learning to weave cultural elements, technologies and political-economic structures to suit the individual requires a detailed understanding of our relationship with the meme. This, in turn, requires the consideration of two key factors: the degree to which we have the ability to use memes freely without creating a dependence on them, and the related power-relationships we must accept in order to utilize selected memes, such as certain technologies. A simple symbolic model suggested by French philosophers Giles Deleuze and Felix Guatari presents a means of harnessing memetic structures without depending on them: the concept of rhizome versus hierarchy.[1] Rhizome provides us with another example of a proven, evolutionarily successful pattern. It acts as the counterpart to, and in many ways is the opposite of, the pattern of hierarchy.

Examples exist throughout history of oppressed peoples, fed up with the tres-passes of hierarchy, revolting in order to establish a new order that will place their interests above those of the existing elite. Over time, hierarchal structures have evolved impressive defenses against such direct assault. Successful revolutions have created their own hierarchal structure to confront strength with strength, but in the process they have sacrificed the objectives—the desire to benefit those at the bottom of the pyramid—that led to revolt in the first place. History dem-onstrates, and common sense validates, that the assumption of hierarchal struc-ture invalidates the actions of groups that would overthrow hierarchy.[2] Despite this logical truism, revolution after revolution proceed along the same path: revo-lutionaries assume hierarchal form to confront the strengths of hierarchies. The

---

1. The concept of Rhizome versus Hierarchy, first presented as a model relevant to human society by Giles Deleuze and Felix Guatari in their book "A Thousand Pla-teaus: Capitalism and Schizophrenia".

[handwritten margin note at top: "in domination principle that's support and is supported by hierarchy"]

solution to hierarchy lies not in the failure of proper implementation (the standard critique of Marxist failures by Marxists), but in the fundamental structure of hierarchy itself. In order to resolve the deficiencies fundamental to the structure of hierarchy, we must, by definition, abandon hierarchy as an organizing principle. We must confront hierarchy with its opposite: rhizome.

Rhizome acts as a web-like structure of connected but independent nodes, borrowing its name from the structures of plants such as bamboo and other grasses. By its very nature, rhizome exhibits incompatibility with such critical hierarchal structures as domestication, monoculture-agriculture, division of labor and centralized government. Unlike hierarchy, rhizome cannot suffer exploitation from within because its structure remains incompatible with centralization of power. It provides a structural framework for our conscious organization of memes. Each node in a rhizome stands autonomous from the larger structure, but the nodes work together in a larger network that extends benefits to the node without creating dependence. The critical element of a world that focuses power at the level of the individual, that can meet the demands of our genome while providing the flexibility and potential to achieve greater goals, remains the small, connected and relatively self-sufficient node of this rhizome structure. In human terms, such a node represents an economic and a cultural unit at the size preferred by our genome: the household and the tribe. Functionally self-sufficient but not isolated, cooperating but not controlled, the rhizome economy, combined with a self-awareness of control structures, provides the real-world foundation of stability and freedom.

[handwritten margin notes: "But why mutual cooperation? motivation? That means all of them."]

Rhizome structure has no inherent instability, but it will quickly reorder into hierarchy if we do not address the institutions within our society that serve to perpetuate hierarchy. The abstract notion of ownership serves as the single, greatest perpetuator of hierarchy. When one steps back and examines the notion of "owning" something, the abstraction becomes readily apparent. Ownership represents nothing more than a power-relationship—the ability to control. The tribal institution of "Ownership by use" on the other hand, suggests simply that one can only "own" those things that they put to immediate, direct and personal

[handwritten note: "PRIVATE PROPERTY"]

---

2. Interestingly, a recent DARPA/RAND report proposed that the US security functions adopt a rhizome-form in order to fight the rhizomatic Al Qaeda: "Defeating networked terrorists probably requires sophisticated network in response." ("Deterrence and Influence in Counterterrorism" by Paul Davis and Brian Jenkins, 2002) What effect will this have on America's hierarchal government?

[handwritten note at bottom: "foundation of the dominating civilization"]

use to meet basic needs—and not more. A society crosses the memetic Rubicon when it accepts the abstraction that ownership can extend beyond the exclusive needs of one individual for survival. Abstract ownership begins when society accepts a claim of symbolic control of something without the requirement of immediate, direct and personal use. Hierarchy, at any level, requires this excess, abstract ownership—it represents the symbolic capital that forms the foundation of all stratification. In the simplest terms, in order to destroy the engine of hierarchy, we must destroy the mechanism of ownership. Proposing to destroy ownership may seem impractical, but societies have achieved similar feats before—such as the!Kung tribe's aversion to status. If a society accepts that hierarchy fails the needs of human ontogeny, then one can argue that ownership—the engine of hierarchy—acts detrimentally to human needs. Like the!Kung taboo on status, a taboo on ownership would represent a serious defeat for hierarchy and all that it represents.

In order to exploit the weakening of hierarchy, hierarchal structures should be replaced with institutionalized rhizome structures in our economic, political and social systems. Society must develop a way to shift from the pattern of self-intensifying hierarchy to the pattern of self-intensifying rhizome. The Roman Late Republic[3] provides an illustrative example from history of one attempt to institutionalize a rhizome-creating process, and the violent backlash of hierarchy—a backlash made possible by the construct of ownership.

While in its earliest days Rome took the form of a kingdom, it quickly transitioned to a quasi-democratic republic. Much of the history of social and political struggle in the Late Republic revolves around the distribution—the de facto ownership—of land. The *populares*, or populist politicians such as Tiberius Grachi, attempted to affect a more even distribution of land through a variety of land reform acts. In opposition to Grachi and others, the *optimates*, rich aristocrats and landholders, attempted to destroy democratic institutions that encouraged reform. The retirement system of the Roman military represented one land-reform battleground. The *populares* instituted a retirement payment in the form of a small plot of agricultural land sufficient to set up a family farm. Over time the process created a populace consisting of largely small, independent landholders. It created rhizome *institutionally*, causing a steady demographic shift as it took poor, landless veterans and made them independent small-farmers. The land-at-retirement system created a stable, rhizome-like network of loyal but

---

3.   The Late Republic is generally defined as 130 to 40 B.C.E.

independent citizens across the countryside. The fabric of small landholders served as the backbone of the Republic; they understood that the glory of Rome represented their glory, the security of Rome represented their security, etc. Land ownership made them citizens, giving them the right to participate in democratic government. They did not see their *civitus*, or sense of civic duty and participation as a burden, but rather as a privilege.

The *optimates* saw the great threat to their privilege posed by the retirement system. They struck back (usually by murdering the reformers), eliminating the land-payment system and providing instead a cash payment insufficient to purchase farm land. Cash payments permitted the re-concentration of wealth in the hands of an elite few. The *optimates* continued to gather land-wealth into a few, huge *latifundia* plantations, reducing the once independent small-farmers to farmhands. The story of land reform and consolidation, rhizome versus hierarchy, defines the story of the fall of the Republic and the rise of Empire.[4]

The student of history will quickly identify similarities between the recent history of the United States and the events that led to the rise of Empire in Rome. If we would like to avoid the fate of Rome—or more pessimistically if we would like to reverse it—then we must create institutionalized systems of self-intensifying rhizome. The institutionalization of systems that create rhizome represents a transition phase, but ultimately we must achieve rhizome without any of the trappings of hierarchy. By its fundamental nature, we must implement rhizome in a bottom-up mode. Institutional—in other words, centralized—means of creating rhizome exist primarily to replace or eliminate those structures that would create hierarchy. The real work of building rhizome must happen at the lowest level, the level of the individual.

Power remains distributed to the level of the individual rhizome node through local, functional self-sufficiency—a modern equivalent to the Domestic Mode of Production. In other words, functional self-sufficiency means the ability to produce at the household level at least the minimum necessities for day-to-day existence without relying on outside agents or resources. Self-sufficiency removes the individual rhizome node from dependence on the standard set of outside suppliers. It does not eliminate exchange, but creates a situation where any exchange exists as a voluntary activity. The commodities that each node must provide for

---

4.   The struggles of the populares and the optimates are chronicled in Michael Parenti's excellent book, *The Assassination of Julius Caesar: A People's History of Ancient Rome.*

But one need first accept voluntary simplicity, reject ~~pro~~ consumerism, need ~~acdolic?~~ to run

itself include staple foodstuffs, energy for heating, basic habitat and small group interaction. With necessary items secured, the node has freedom to pursue a vision without being dependent on external, self-motivated entities.

COMMUNITY

Many will balk at the prospect of achieving functional self-sufficiency. Those of us who live in the global industrial economy have largely lost the knowledge of our ancestors—the knowledge required to support ourselves. Likewise, many will point out that so-called "green" initiatives, such as photovoltaic cells, hybrid cars, collective housing, etc. have failed to prove their economic viability without heavy subsidies. Such "green" initiatives serve as nothing more than symbolic, token efforts by an economic structure committed to centralization. Remove the demand of centralized production, and several simple, viable paths exist to reach self-sufficiency. These paths do not require a reduction in quality of life. In fact, if we use a measurement methodology based on our ontogeny, they provide dramatic quality of life increases.

It all depends on what we value

We require energy, for example, for heating, cooling, cooking, communications, etc. Electricity, when honestly examined, provides an extremely inefficient solution to our energy needs. The ease with which the economy can centralize production and distribution of electricity, however, makes it the method of choice. Consider the inefficiencies: solar energy converts to one of a variety of fossil fuels (coal, oil, timber, etc.) over time. Energy corporations then expend enormous resources to gather that fuel from naturally dispersed positions to a centralized location. Then, using incredibly inefficient processes which create toxic wastes, they combust the fuel and convert the resulting heat into electricity. Using expensive transmission lines they distribute the electricity, with a great loss in the process. Finally, consumers convert the electricity back into heat (in most cases) using, again, incredibly inefficient processes. This represents a staggering combined inefficiency, but does permit centralized control of electricity, as well as the (non-electrical) power associated with it.[5] If we reject the need to centralize this process, we can quite easily harness all the energy that we need on our own. Passive solar heating and cooling design converts sunlight directly into heat, without any of the compounded inefficiencies described above. Designers around the world have demonstrated the viability of passive solar to provide for all heating, cooling and cooking needs using nothing more than locally available materials. The vernacular architecture of "primitive" peoples around the world provides

---

5.   See "Energy, Society and Hierarchy" by the author, at http://www.directactionjournal.org/energy.html

Distributed system.

hard proof of this. While a complete how-to manual of passive solar design reaches beyond the scope of this text, ample resources are easily available to provide instruction.[6] Why, then, do governments and corporations not tout passive solar as the solution to the world's energy and environmental problems? Again, this results from the impossibility of centralizing control over passive solar. Only the photovoltaic cell has received any significant level of support from government or industry—because its manufacture requires centralization.

Similarly, food production appears daunting to most suburbanites at first glance. Several innovative methods exist, however, that can provide a family with superior nutrition from spaces often as small as a suburban lot. Not surprisingly, these methods look to the rhizome-structure of nature, and the techniques of our hunter-gatherer ancestors for inspiration. The most widespread of these, the Permaculture method created by Bill Mollison and David Holmgren provides techniques for perennial, ecology-based agricultural food production. Perhaps more exciting, the methods of Masanobu Fukuoka essentially advocate setting up a concentrated gathering ecology, eliminating the need for the labor of agriculture, while providing exceptionally high yields.[7] As pioneers begin to demonstrate the viability, even the preferability of such decentralized methods of self-sufficiency, the strength of the rhizome network will grow.

With a foundation of self-sufficiency established, a node can take advantage of a second strength of the rhizome pattern: network. Loose network connections, such as those in rhizome structures, actually demonstrate far more efficiency at information transfer and processing than the close, authoritarian connections of hierarchies, according to complexity theorist Mark Buchanan.[8] The more intense, closely held connections within hierarchy prevent information from quickly spreading among large or diverse groups. The weaker, more distributed

---

6. Most book stores carry several volumes covering passive solar design, straw bale and other alternative building methods, greywater design, etc. Books on vernacular architecture, such as "A Shelter Sketchbook" by John S. taylor, "Architecture Without Architects" by Bernard Rudofsky and "Shelter" by Bob Easton and Lloyd Khan provide an especially underutilized resource.

7. See "Permaculture: A Designer's Manual" by Bill Mollison, "Permaculture: Principles and Pathways Beyond Sustainability" by David Holmgren, "The Natural Way of Farming" and "The One-Straw Revolution" by Masanobu Fukuoka, as well as the website http://www.seedballs.com

8. "Nexus: Small Worlds and the Groundbreaking Theory of Networks", Mark Buchanan.

connections of a network can more quickly disseminate information to a much broader audience:

> If…ten students had started some rumor that moved only between the best friends, it would have infected their own social group, but not much more. In contrast, a rumor moving along weaker links would go much farther (to more diverse social groupings). As in the case of people seeking jobs, information spreading along weak ties has a better chance to reach a large number of people.[9]

Wilson's SNAFU principle[10] serves as a Corollary to this theory of the power of weak connections: the integrity of information degrades every time it relays from one point to another—sociologically in the manner of the children's game "telephone",[11] and physically through signal attenuation. Hierarchies become inefficient at information processing as they intensify because the number of close-proximity relays that information must cross to reach from the bottom to the top of the hierarchy quickly mushrooms. Furthermore, Wilson's SNAFU principle states that the one-directional power-relationships of hierarchy introduce additional, intentional distortion at every relay: underlings skew information to tell their bosses what they want to hear. This process repeats again and again as information works its way up the ladder until eventually the top of the hierarchy has no clue what happens at the bottom. This results in forcing hierarchies to dedicate an ever-larger share of available resources to maintain internal communications, as anyone who has ever worked for a government or large corporation can readily attest. Networks of small, independent nodes introduce far less attenuation or distortion in information processing, compensating for their inability to stratify or exert command-and-control to the same degree as hierarchies.

In order to leverage the strength of network, we must undertake voluntary communication and information exchange, partnership-based exchange in locally specialized commodities and services, as well as broader cultural interactions between networks of rhizome nodes. Such interaction can provide many of the

---

9. "Nexus: Small Worlds and the Groundbreaking Theory of Networks", Mark Buchanan., pg 46.
10. R. A. Wilson's SNAFU principle, proposing the existence of an "information jam in hierarchy", is discussed in several of his books, including "The Illuminati Papers".
11. Telephone is a game where a message is passed, one person at a time, down a line of children. Normally the message reaching the end of the line bears very little resemblance to the original.

benefits of traditional hierarchal economies and political entities without relegating the participant nodes to a subservient relationship. They participate voluntarily, as equals—a status maintained due to the self-awareness of each node regarding the dangers of abandoning their rhizome structure in favor of stratification and hierarchy. Self-sufficient, local nodes, in combination with a few weaker, long-distance links to other nodes create information-processing and economic powerhouses—not recognizable in the contemporary, industrial sense, but instead as vibrant beacons of human potential and fulfillment. Modeled after the same architecture that makes the human brain so powerful, such a system does not represent a return to the Stone Age. Rather, this mirrors the exact architecture, the "small world" theory of networks[12] that cutting edge economists and management gurus would love to implement—if only they could figure out a way to keep the benefits flowing into the hands of the favored few. Rhizome economies, in contrast, utilize this "small world" theory to maintain efficiency and information flow while keeping power concentrated in the hands of the many.

The field of ecology provides further insight into the comparison of hierarchy versus rhizome. Greater diversity and complexity in an ecosystem increases its resiliency. The rigid stratification of hierarchy, while efficient from the standpoint of centralized control and coordination, has proved less capable of supporting dense, stable networks of organic life (of which humanity remains a part). Centralization and stratification produce ever-greater losses in efficiency due to the increased cost of distribution, coordination and communication. Hierarchy has incredible strength, but the accompanying inflexibility and top-heaviness can make it brittle and unstable. The networked, rhizome structure not only facilitates greater individual freedom, it also creates a more flexible and resilient structure for human ecology. The resiliency of rhizome may prove the deciding factor in our long-term survival as humanity encounters a host of potential threats. In the face of super-viruses, climate-change and overpopulation, the richer, more complex, more rhizomatic ecosystem has historically demonstrated greater survivability.

Despite the potential to establish independence through alternative economic and cultural structures, we can only achieve true independence in a society that conquers the problem of physical power. A group free from economic or cultural control by an outside agent can still suffer control through force.[13] Remnant

---

12. "Nexus: Small Worlds and the Groundbreaking Theory of Networks", Mark Buchanan, pg. 208.

hunter-gatherer tribes in the Amazon illustrate the limitations of self-sufficiency. They do not exhibit dependency on the outside world for anything, yet logging companies and ranchers with access to greater physical force (in the form of the State) have repeatedly forced them off their land.

The case of the Branch Davidians of Waco, Texas provides a more relevant example for most members of industrial society.[14] Regardless of one's interpretation of the event, the siege and destruction of the Branch Davidian complex occurred when the group attempted to achieve independence without realistically addressing the problem of physical power: how to prevent physical control by an outside group. They recognized the need to address the issue of physical power, but their failure embodied the mistakes of a long history of failed revolutions. Their static and defensive position, combined with the tactic of confronting firepower with firepower, played directly to the strengths of their hierarchal opponent. If the strength of hierarchy exists in confronting symmetrical, frontal assaults, then its weakness lies in Antonio Negri's concept of "diagonal".[15] The current rise to prominence of one manifestation of such a "diagonal", asymmetrical approach—normally mislabeled as "terrorism"—has barely scratched the surface of the multitude of possible tactics in confronting hierarchy, in addressing the problem of physical power.

We can address physical power in one of only three fundamental ways. One can prevent another power from dominating due to their 1) lack of relative physical strength, 2) lack of desire to dominate, or 3) failure to recognize the opportunity to dominate. The first solution, being stronger than all potential dominators, remains unrealistic for the immediate future. Semi-rhizome structures, such as the American militias of the 1770s can defeat a powerful hierarchy like the British army. This approach, however, requires a readiness for physical confrontation and mobilization of a large rhizome structure. Historically, the mobilization of rhizome polities (American militias, Gallic tribes, etc.) to defeat a state resulted in the amalgamation of this rhizome into the same kind of hierarchal state structure

---

13. For a cautionary tale that points out both the potential of rhizome as well as the danger of ignoring the problem of power, see *Island* by Aldous Huxley.
14. The Bureau of Alcohol, Tobacco and Firearms destroyed the Branch Davidian complex on April 19th, 1993. Controversy continues over the exact sequence of events. Consider the film *Rules of Engagement* and the collection of essays *Against Civilization* by John Zerzan for alternative interpretations of the incident.
15. See *Empire* by Antonio Negri and Michael Hardt

Common! This cannot be imagined

that they were fighting, defeating the purpose of their coalition. In the example of the American Revolution, it seems likely that the second solution, lack of desire to dominate, may have finally decided the conflict. Had the British Empire decided to mobilize all resources, at all costs, to defeat the colonists, a far different outcome may have resulted. This more "diagonal" tactic, addressing the desire of an outside power to dominate, exists as a highly effective solution to the problem of power. Many of today's remnant hunter-gatherers have stumbled upon this solution. Their inhabitation of marginal territory, such as the tribes of the Kalahari Desert, creates a situation where no outside power wants what they have. Finally, it remains possible to prevent domination by making the rhizome invisible to an outside power. If the sensory apparatus of a state or other power fails to detect something, it seems far less likely to succeed in dominating it.[16] Examples include the Romani gypsies of Europe and North America, 1960's 'Back to the Land' communes, individuals who operate exclusively in a cash economy, etc. Hakim Bey, self-described "guerilla ontologist", has proposed a variety of "Autonomous Zone" concepts, from temporary festivals to permanent settlements, which explore the invisibility of some structures to the eyes of the state.[17] The approach of invisibility may represent the most realistic solution to the problem of power, at least until the size of a rhizome network provides enough political or physical power to make the other options realistic. In his last, and perhaps finest novel, *Island*, Aldous Huxley provides a powerful warning to those who would work to foster rhizome: physical power is the Achilles Heel of any society that wishes to work within the bounds of human ontogeny—we must not ignore this lesson.

I hope that with a new awareness of the structure of our world, along with a growing enlightenment regarding our sense of self, we will experience an increasing movement to live in harmony with our genetic requirements—an archaic revival. A new vision, with individual freedom to pursue arts and spirituality, above the pettiness of bickering for power, may prove possible if we learn to control the powers that have dominated us throughout history. In the spirit of this vision, the message will ultimately fail if forced upon others. Only through *personal example*, by showing that a realistic and preferable alternative exists, will these concepts succeed on a large scale. We will act as pioneers, who will begin to

---

16. "Seeing Like a State", James C. Scott.
17. Most of the works of Hakim Bey are freely available at http://www.hermetic.com/bey/. Specifically, see *Temporary Autonomous Zone*, *Periodic Autonomous Zone*, and *Permanent Autonomous Zone*.

create diverse rhizome nodes, each one representing an individual's struggle to solve the problems of hierarchy and human ontogeny. The more we learn and break free from the control of genes and memes, the more success these pioneers will have. Effective tools and practices will spread, and the rhizome network will grow and strengthen. As this network evolves, it will provide a realistic, implementable alternative to hierarchy—an alternative that fulfills our genetic ontogeny and empowers us as individuals. Nature has shown us that the structure of the rhizome can compete with hierarchy and stratification. When combined with an understanding of reality and humanity that makes us our own masters, we may finally learn from the events of the past…and gain control of our future.

meanwhile, we will have a major breakdown, "long emergency", a collapse of civilization.

we need to have some example, some patterns to turn to.

All such work toward a different future, eyeing the system of our civilization is priceless.

References

For a digital list of references and footnotes with hypertext links, visit **www.jeffvail.net**

Alcock, John. *The Triumph of Sociobiology*, Oxford University Press, 2001.

Bandler, Richard and Grinder, John. *The Structure of Magic: A Book About Language and Therapy*, Science and Behavior Books, 1975.

Bey, Hakim. *Temporary Autonomous Zone*, Autonomedia.

Bey, Hakim. *Periodic Autonomous Zone*, Autonomedia.

Bey, Hakim. *Permanent Autonomous Zone*, Autonomedia.

Blackmore, Susan. *The Meme Machine*, Oxford University Press, 1999.

Bloom, Howard. *Global Brain*, Wiley, 2000.

Brown, Lester R. *Eco-Economy: Building An Economy for the Earth*, W.W. Norton & Co., 2001.

Buchanan, Mark. *Nexus: Small Worlds and the Groundbreaking Theory of Networks*, W.W. Norton & Co., 2002.

Camazine, Scott, et al. *Self-Organization in Biological Systems*, Princeton University Press, 2001.

Caton-Thompson, Gertrude. *Mixed Memoirs*, Erskine Press, 1983.

Dawkins, Richard. *The Selfish Gene*, Oxford University Press, 1979.

De Landa, Manuel. *1000 Years of Non-Linear History*, MIT Press, 1997.

Deleuze, Giles and Guattari, Felix. *A Thousand Plateaus: Capitalism and Schizophrenia*, trans. Brian Massumi, University of Minnesota Press, 1987.

Diamond, Jared. *Guns, Germs, and Steel: The Fates of Human Societies*, W.W. Norton & Co., 1997.

Donald, Merlin. *Origins of the Modern Mind*, Harvard University Press, 1991.

Earle, Timothy K. *Bronze Age Economics*, Westview Press, 2002.

Easton, Bob and Khan, Lloyd. *Shelter*, Shelter Publications, 1973.

Ellul, Jacques. *The Technological Society*, Vintage Books USA, 1967.

Feynman, Richard P. *QED: The Strange Theory of Light and Matter*, Princeton University Press, 1986.

Fukuoka, Masanobu. *The Natural Way of Farming*, Kodansha, 1985.

Fukuyama, Francis. *Our Posthuman Future*, Farrar Straus Grioux, 2002

Hall, Manly P. *The Secret Teachings of All Ages*, Philosophical Research Society, 1978.

Harris, Marvin. *Cows, Pigs, Wars and Witches*, Random House, 1974.

Hartmann, Thom. *Whose Disorder is Being Disordered by ADHD*, from http://www.thomhartmann.com/

Holland, John. *A Hidden Order*, Perseus Books Group, 1995.

Holmgren, David. *Permaculture: Principles and Pathways Beyond Sustainability*, Holmgren Design Services, 2002.

Huxley, Aldous. *Island*, Harper Collins, 1962.

Huxley, Aldous. *The Perennial Philosophy*, Borgo Press, 1990.

Johnson, Steven. *Mind Wide Open*, Scribner, 2004.

Kirch, Patrick V. *On the Road of the Winds*, University of California Press, 2000.

Lee, Richard B. *The Dobe Ju/'hoansi*, Wadsworth Publishing, 2002.

McTaggart, Lynne. *The Field*, Harper Collins, 2002.

Mollison, Bill. *Permaculture: A Designer's Manual*, Tagari Publications, 1997.

Negri, Antonio and Hardt, Michael. *Empire*, Harvard University Press, 2000.

Novak, Robert. *Anarchy, State and Utopia*, Basic Books, 1974.

Parenti, Michael. *The Assassination of Julius Caesar: A People's History of Ancient Rome*, New Press, 2003.

Quinn, Daniel. *Beyond Civilization*, Random House, 1999.

Rudofsky, Bernard. *Architecture Without Architects*, University of New Mexico Press, 1987.

Sahlins, Marshal. *Stone Age Economics*, Aldine de Gruyter, 1972.

Shuman, Michael. *Going Local*, Free Press, 1998.

Scott, James C. *Seeing Like a State: How Certain Schemes to Improve the Human Condition Have Failed*, Yale University Press, 1998.

Shepard, Paul and Shepard, Florence. *Coming Home to the Pleistocene*, Shearwater Books, 1998

Shepard, Paul. *Traces of an Omnivore*, Shearwater, 1996.

Sober, E. and Wilson, D. S. *Unto Others: The Evolution and Psychology of Unselfish Behavior*, Harvard University Press, 1998.

Taylor, John S. *A Shelter Sketchbook: Timeless Building Solutions*, Chelsea Green 1997.

Thurston, Harry. *Secrets of the Sands: Revelations of Egypt's Everlasting Oasis*, Arcade Books, 2004.

Wilson, Edward O. *Consilience: The Unity of Knowledge*, Knopf, 1998.

Wilson, Robert Anton. *Cosmic Trigger*, New Falcon, 1991.

Wilson, Robert Anton. *Prometheus Rising*, New Falcon, 1992.

Wilson, Robert Anton. *Quantum Psychology*, New Falcon, 1990.

Zee, Anthony. *Quantum Field Theory in a Nutshell*, Princeton University Press, 2003.

Zerzan, John. *Against Civilization: Readings and Reflections*, Uncivilized Books, 1999.

Zerzan, John. *Future Primitive & Other Essays*, Autonomedia, 1994.

What I take from
this book?

- Intensification
- we must first control ourselve
  and then figure out how
  to control power relationship

- change must occur at the
  level that it worked. Small individual
  groups (family, band, tribe
  = community. Self-sufficie

- ownership (private property)
  foundation of hierarchy,
  of IPC enabler
  owning = controlling
  only things that are necessary t
  Individual's survival

- Distributed systems & diversi
  Resilience.

- The ultimate goal is to cont
  forces that dominate humani
  starting from self.

- Invisible to outside po
  mycelium

0-595-33030-4

when hunt/gather we sacrifice and
grew in number, they just could
move further and didn't create
population pressure. Or, were
there dependent on Nature cycles
More bison → more people

with agriculture, people could not
move away. They might only inc
their way to expand.

Transition? It must be
through organizations!
Ultimately, yes. Small to self-su
unit

Printed in the United States
40599LVS00005B/284

9 780595 330300